0404114

W9-BYU-070

ON LINE

FOOTBALL HALL OF FAMERS

JOE MONTANA

Fred Ramen

the rosen publishing group's
rosen
central

To Douglas Berry, who remembers where he was when Dwight Clark made The Catch

Published in 2003 by The Rosen Publishing Group, Inc.
29 East 21st Street, New York, NY 10010

Library of Congress Cataloging-in-Publication Data

Ramen, Fred.
Joe Montana / Fred Ramen.—1st ed.
    p. cm.—(Football hall of famers)
ISBN 0-8239-3607-4 (lib. bdg.)
1. Montana, Joe, 1956– —Juvenile literature. 2. Football players—United States—Biography—Juvenile literature.
[1. Montana, Joe, 1956– 2. Football players.]
I. Title. II. Series.
GV939.M59 R36 2003
796.332'092—dc21

2001006631

Manufactured in the United States of America

Contents

Quarterback Joe Montana ended his career with impressive statistics: 40,551 yards, 3,409 completions, 273 touchdowns, 4 Super Bowl victories, 3 MVP titles, and 1 town named for him. That's not bad for someone who had 81 players picked ahead of him in the 1979 NFL draft.

Introduction

Standing just over six feet tall and usually weighing less than 195 pounds, Joe Montana never seemed like the ideal quarterback. He had spindly legs and a slight build, though he had rugged good looks and intense blue eyes. He never ran very fast, although he had excellent reflexes, making him harder to tackle than one might think. His arm was good by NFL standards but never great; it wasn't his style to heave the ball 40 or 50 yards upfield as John Elway or Dan Marino did. However, nobody in history has ever been a more accurate passer.

Montana would calmly roll out to zip short pass after short pass into the teeth of the opposing defense, chewing away little pieces of territory until everything would break the right way.

Montana prepares for a pass during Super Bowl XXIV against the Denver Broncos in 1990, which the 49ers won. Known to many as Joe Cool or the Comeback Kid, Montana engineered 31 fourth-quarter comebacks in his magnificent NFL career.

Suddenly, a fleeing man in a San Francisco 49ers uniform would be all alone and running for the goal line, clutching a ball delivered to him only a moment before.

This football great from Monongahela, Pennsylvania, won every Super Bowl game he ever played in—four of them—and helped to establish the San Francisco 49ers as the best football team of the 1980s and early 1990s, a sports dynasty overshadowed only by basketball's Chicago Bulls. This leader would go on to be a legendary football player and was eventually inducted into the Pro Football Hall of Fame—an honor reserved for the greatest of the greats.

The
Comeback Kid

Joseph C. Montana Jr. was born on June 11, 1956, in the western Pennsylvania town of New Eagle, just outside Mononga-hela. He was the only child of Joe and Theresa Montana. Even as a very young boy, he displayed remarkable physical abilities. His mother recalled that he nearly destroyed his crib by standing up in it and rocking the sides back and forth. Sometimes he even managed to climb out of the crib and run to his parents' bed.

Father and Son

From an early age, Joe played with his father: catch, one-on-one basketball, and especially football. It soon became obvious that the younger Montana had the makings of a talented athlete. Joe's family had always been athletic.

His grandfather, "Hooks" Montana, had been good enough to play minor league football during the 1920s. And Joe's father was an excellent all-around athlete who had played many different sports (but especially baseball) during his time in the navy. Young Joe also inherited his father's competitive spirit. Most important, the senior Montana encouraged his son to play any and every sport. After school, father and son would go next door to the neighbor's yard and Joe would toss a football through a tire swing that his father would push back and forth. Trying to hit such a small, moving target forced Joe to develop the superb reflexes and instincts he would later bring to the 49ers.

Football, Basketball, Baseball ...

The Montanas played catch—Joe pitched and his father caught—in the alley between their house and the neighbor's. They also played basketball using the hoop Joe's father put over the garage door. And, as Joe got older, he moved into organized sports: Little League, Pee Wee Football, and various school teams.

Like the children in the above photo, Montana played on a Pee Wee football team. Usually, these teams are privately organized and raise their own funds.

Never a Quitter

When Joe was 10 years old, he had had enough of constantly playing sports all year long. He wanted to quit football and join the Boy Scouts. His father told him that he could stop playing if he wanted to, but first he had to finish the season; he didn't want Joe to think that he could quit something he had started. Eventually, Joe finished the season, but he never did join the Scouts. In the coming years, many teams would learn that Joe never quit any game he started.

Slam-Dunk Joe

Joe grew up a multiple-sports star. He was a phenomenal pitcher who threw three perfect games in Little League. In the winter, after the football season, he played basketball. There had been no organized basketball program in his town until Joe's father started one, putting up his own money and running the practices. The team played in tournaments all across the Northeast. On one occasion, they played one night in Bethel Park, Pennsylvania, the following night in Niagara Falls, New York, and then returned to Bethel Park the next night.

Players and fans alike remember Joe as a fantastic basketball player with an amazing vertical leap. It may be hard to believe, but he would actually compete in slam-dunk contests in high school and college. One high school teammate was most impressed by his competitiveness in one-on-one games: "I've seen him play one-on-one, spot some guy eight points, and beat him, 10–8. Beat him with his left hand," Brian Phillips, Montana's junior high school center, recalled in an article in *The Sporting News*.

Montana grew up near the Monongahela River. Because of factories like the one shown here, the river is the second most polluted river in Pennsylvania.

Young Montana was so good that at the end of his high school career, the University of North Carolina—long known for its powerhouse basketball teams (Michael Jordan later played there)—offered him a scholarship. But football was Joe's main sport, the one in which he believed he had a future. From the very start, when his father lied about Joe's age to get him into Pee Wee Football a year early, Joe played quarterback. And very soon he was the heart of the offense of any team on which he played. Many of Joe's teammates agree that the talents he would one day display in four Super Bowls were there from the beginning of his career: the incredible instinct for knowing when a player would get open; the phenomenal accuracy and touch of his arm; and the confidence that if his team had any chance at all, Joe would find a way to win. In those days, before the

Where the Great Ones Are

For the last several decades, a strange thing has happened: Some of the greatest quarterbacks in the history of football have emerged from western Pennsylvania. George Blanda, who passed (and kicked) for several teams in a career that lasted more than two decades, is from Youngswood. Joe Namath, the "Broadway Joe" of the New York Jets who, by backing up his startling guarantee of victory in Super Bowl III, may have forced the merger of the National Football League and the American Football League, is from Beaver Falls. Dan Marino, who has practically rewritten the record book during his astonishing career, is from Pittsburgh. The

Continued on next page

Continued from previous page

Steel City was also home to Johnny Unitas, whom many consider the greatest quarterback in the history of the NFL. His career began in the 1950s and lasted so long that he played against Namath in the 1969 Super Bowl.

Legendary quarterbacks, all from western Pennsylvania. *Clockwise from top left:* the Chicago Bears' George Blanda throws warm-up passes in 1954, a 1957 picture of Johnny Unitas of the Baltimore Colts, the Miami Dolphins' Dan Marino, the New York Jets' Joe Namath.

injuries that plagued him in college and the pros, Joe was also fast; he was capable of scrambling free to pick up a first down. And his trademark move was already in place. It was known as rolling out of the pocket. Joe would move to his right or left, past the protection of his offensive lineman in order to get off a quick pass past the area controlled by the defense.

The Monongahela Valley Tradition

As a quarterback at Ringgold High School, Joe was following in the tradition of many other Monongahela Valley residents, such as football greats George Blanda and Dan Marino. Western Pennsylvania can be hard country. At one time, it was one of the nation's biggest coal- and steel-producing areas. The people who lived there were tough-minded, no-nonsense men and women, people accustomed to hardship, people who believed in the virtues of hard work and discipline.

While Joe played at Ringgold, he and Coach Chuck Abramski had a stormy relationship. There were two reasons for this: the coach's weight program and how little playing time Abramski gave Joe. The weight-training program was a big part of Coach Abramski's success at Ringgold. In his opinion, it was a good way of bringing the players together as a team, as well as toughening them up and getting them in shape for the season. He scheduled the weight program for the end of summer before the school year began, a time when most of his players were free. The workouts, which were structured and supervised by Abramski, provided excellent training and gave the players a chance to get to know one another and grow accustomed to their coach's leadership style.

Trouble in the Locker Room

The problem was that Joe Montana, the superstar who would take over the team as its quarterback in his junior year, didn't show up for the program. He had other commitments; he was playing American Legion baseball and summer basketball. He played sports all year long and didn't want to take off from competing in a sport in order to be bothered by weight

Montana lets it all sink in after he leads his team to his first Super Bowl victory in 1982. Montana finished his career with four Super Bowl triumphs. Terry Bradshaw of the Pittsburgh Steelers is the only other quarterback to win as many Super Bowls.

training. At the time, it was not completely clear that his future lay in professional football. After all, many people who knew him then say that he was a better basketball player than he was a football player.

As did many of the coaches Joe played for, Abramski may have initially underestimated Joe. After all, western Pennsylvania breeds big, tough quarterbacks. Here was a six-foot-tall sophomore weighing only 165 pounds. It didn't seem likely that he would survive the rough-and-tumble world of western Pennsylvania high school football. Joe got a seat on the bench, where he watched how the program was run and received orders to report to the coach's summer weight-training program.

Benched

When Joe's junior year began, he was still on the bench. This would not be the last time he was passed over for less talented players, but it bothered him then, just as it would later bother him in college football at Notre Dame and in the pros. Instead of using Joe's uncanny passing touch and superior scrambling ability to win games, Ringgold tried to win behind big Paul Timko, a strong young man who could hit defenders like a brick wall but who probably couldn't hit the same brick wall when he threw the ball. Ringgold lost the opener with Timko as quarterback in a blowout and then won two forfeits caused by a teachers' strike.

It was obvious that Timko wasn't going to lead the Ringgold Rams to a state title, so Joe took over the quarterback position during practice. It was rough, especially because Timko had been moved to defensive end and tried to splatter Joe on every play. But when regular play resumed, Joe was the quarterback and Timko had been moved to tight end—and now, when Timko needed the ball, Joe was suddenly one of his best friends.

Then a legendary battle began, between Ringgold High and Monessen High, a local powerhouse known for being tough and nasty. The team would be playing on the road, and nobody—except Joe Montana—thought Ringgold had much of a chance. Facing a hostile crowd, Montana led Ringgold to a 21–7 halftime lead, throwing three touchdowns in the first half. He would add another in the second half, but Monessen managed to score on the game's final play, resulting in a 34–34 tie that felt like a win for everybody on the Ringgold team. Three of Joe's four touchdowns had gone to Paul Timko.

From then on, there was nowhere to go but up.

Superstar in the Works

During his final two years at Ringgold, Joe led an explosive offense. His senior team went 8-1 and was a strong contender for a state title until they had a play-off game in a sleet storm with three starters injured and out of the game. Joe was a *Parade* magazine All-American. Scouts from several major colleges had swooped down once more into the Monongahela Valley looking for the next Namath or Unitas. During games, scouts would stand on a

Richard "Digger" Phelps, Notre Dame's famous basketball coach, was eager to have Montana on his team. Montana eventually chose to focus only on football.

lot overlooking the stadium with Joe's father and try to convince him that their school would be best for his son's future.

Young Montana wasn't being wooed only by football programs. The University of North Carolina offered him a basketball scholarship. Notre Dame's famed basketball coach, Digger Phelps, offered to arrange things so that Joe could be a two-sport star—playing basketball and football—at Notre Dame. Joe tried out at a major league baseball camp and was good enough to be invited back. For a while, he seriously considered playing basketball, which had always been lots of fun for him, instead of football.

In the end, perhaps because he was realistic about his chances for success as a six-foot-one-inch basketball player, he decided to pursue a football scholarship. As good as his basketball skills were, and though he really enjoyed the game, his football skills were positively uncanny. The only question was where he would go. Joe visited Boston College, the University of Minnesota, and Notre Dame. The University of Pittsburgh was practically his hometown team, so he was already familiar with them; but he also visited Penn State. A scout for the University of Georgia offered Joe a scholarship after watching him practice.

But in the end, there really wasn't any choice. Joe Montana would follow his dream and head to the golden dome of Notre Dame.

Notre Dame

Growing up, Joe Montana had many idols among the quarterbacks who had come from the Monongahela Valley. Joe Namath, with his deadly arm and amazing ability to lead his team to victory, was one. Another was Terry Hanratty, a player who is much less well known today. Hanratty had gone to Notre Dame and won a national title under the great coach Ara Parseghian the year before Joe arrived at the university.

Big Changes

It is not surprising that Notre Dame was such an attractive place for young Montana. Certainly, it had been a dream of his father's to have his son win a national championship for the Fighting

The Fighting Irish

Notre Dame already had a legendary football program before Joe showed up to add to its accomplishments. From the earliest days of college football, the Fighting Irish of the South Bend, Indiana, university had been one of the top teams. Here, the legendary Four Horsemen—the great offensive backfield of the undefeated 1925 national champion Notre Dame—had galloped across the record books in the days when the helmets were made of leather and football was still a gentleman's sport. Their renowned coach, Knute Rockne, was the first to utilize the forward pass as a part of the offense, forever changing the game of football. Rockne also built a national following for the team by playing games all across the country. For decades, Notre Dame had turned out great teams, producing rosters packed with All-American and Heisman Trophy winners. Many of the other schools that had been powerhouses in the early days of college football had become second-rate teams, such as Army and Princeton, but Notre Dame endured.

Overall, Notre Dame has won the national championship 11 times, more than any other college, and it has produced seven Heisman Trophy winners, also more than any other college. Several legendary NFL players, including Green Bay Packers running back Paul Hornung, the Raiders' wide receiver Tim Brown, and, of course, Joe Montana, played for Notre Dame as well.

The Heisman Memorial Trophy is awarded annually to the most outstanding college football player in the United States. Though Montana had three great seasons with Notre Dame, he never won the trophy.

Irish. But while Joe ultimately succeeded beyond anybody's expectations, for much of his college career, he faced one frustrating setback after another.

One of the first things he had to get used to was being away from home. For a small-town kid, life at a large university was an enormous change. It didn't help that Joe had always been a little shy. At Notre Dame, he initially had trouble making friends. He would call his father several times a week. Joe Sr., quick to respond to his son's homesickness and difficulty settling in, often made unannounced trips to the school, making the eight-hour drive from Monongahela and arriving in the middle of the night to take Joe out for pancakes. Joe was thankful for these visits. In many ways, Joe's father was his best friend during his first years at college.

Another worry for Joe was Notre Dame's tough academic standards. It was a top school, and the teachers, many of whom were Catholic priests, were not willing to give any breaks to football players. Joe found himself in a continual tug-of-war between working on his studies and

working on his football career. During his sophomore year, while he was trying to win the starting
quarterback job, he was on academic probation.

One of Joe's first friends at Notre Dame
was his roommate, Nick DiCicco, who was also
a football player. Nick's father, Mike, was the
school's fencing coach and the academic adviser
to all the football players. Mike's encourage-
ment and support helped Joe with his tough
classes, as well as through his difficult early
years at Notre Dame.

During his freshman year, Joe got married
to his high school sweetheart, Kim Moses.
Unfortunately for the couple, the match was
not a good one, and they divorced less than
three years later.

A number of other changes occurred after
Joe's freshman year. The first was that Ara
Parseghian, the head coach, resigned for health
and personal reasons. The second was that Joe
got off the bench and into a game, with impressive results. Parseghian had been one of the best
coaches in Notre Dame history, leading the
squad to three bowl games and two national

Despite an injury that forced him to sit out his second season at Notre Dame, Montana made an amazing comeback and led his team to two consecutive Cotton Bowl victories. In this picture, Montana makes a gain of six yards in a game against Georgia Tech, which Notre Dame won 69–14.

championships. Joe was sorry to see him go, but there was hope that the new coach, Dan Devine, would want to make a clean start and open up some of the starting jobs. Although it was going to be a challenge, Joe was determined to become the starting quarterback. At the time, Joe was the seventh-string quarterback on the team, but he and Coach Devine never would get along all that well.

Dan Devine, like Chuck Abramski, doubted that Joe could take the pounding of big–time college football. And with so many quarter-backs in the program, it was easy to overlook the youngster from Pennsylvania. Maybe this is why, even after he had some success in college football, Joe had to fight for the starting job.

His first big chance came against North-western. Down 7–0 in the first quarter, starting quarterback Rick Slager was injured and Joe came in to finish off a scoring drive. He stayed in the game, leading the team to three more touchdowns, including his first touchdown pass at Notre Dame and the first touchdown he ran for the school; the Irish won 31–7.

Montana smiles as the clock ticks away the final seconds of the 1978 Cotton Bowl, which Notre Dame won, beating favorite University of Texas by a crushing 38 points to 10.

After that performance, Joe naturally thought he would be the starter the following week. However, it wasn't to be. Northwestern was a school Notre Dame traditionally beat up on; in the eyes of the coaches, perhaps, Joe's performance against them wasn't anything special, it was simply what was expected of him. But that game was not to be Joe's last chance at Notre Dame. Two weeks later, the Irish offense was being stifled by a tough University of North Carolina defense. The Irish were on the road, the temperature was over 90 degrees, and they trailed 14–0 in the fourth quarter. Coach Devine turned to Joe.

He responded with the first of his many "miracle" comebacks. First, he led the Irish on a five-play, 73-yard scoring drive, capping it off with a pass for the two-point conversion. When the Notre Dame defense held off North Carolina, Joe got the ball back on his own 20-yard line with just over a minute left.

The play that left a huge impact on the Irish faithful came on the second down, 10 yards to go from the Notre Dame twenty. There was more than a minute left in the game when Joe called an audible at the line of scrimmage, stepped up and threw to Ted Burgmeier on the sidelines, and then threw up his hands in celebration as the receiver went 80 yards for the game-winning touchdown. Entering the game with five minutes left, Joe had delivered an improbable win. With it, he got the right to start the next game against longtime rivals University of Southern California (USC).

Unfortunately, the results were not what he wanted. Although Joe led his team to a 14–7 halftime lead, the Trojans' ground game was too tough for the Irish, and they won 21–17, with Joe throwing an interception on his last possession. After that, he went back to the bench for a good part of the rest of the season. Even so, he still came in during the fourth quarter of a game the Irish were losing 30–10 to the U.S. Air Force Academy, and he threw two touchdowns to lead Notre Dame to a 31–30 win.

After these heroics, Joe assumed that he would be the starter going into his junior year, especially since Rick Slager was graduating. But Coach Devine did not name a starter. Instead, he let the quarterbacks compete for the starting job. This led to what was thus far the worst moment of Joe's football life.

It came on one of the last plays during the last practice before the season began. The team was working on pushing the ball in from the 10-yard line. The drill had been going on for a while, but Coach Devine told them to keep working on it. Joe took the snap and slipped. As he started to fall, a defender came in unblocked and crunched him into the ground before he could prepare himself. The hit separated Joe's shoulder, and it was the end of the 1976 season for him—he had to sit out the entire year while his shoulder healed.

Rising to the Top

Joe never quite forgave Devine for his first two years at Notre Dame. Several things left him feeling bitter about the experience: the constant struggle for the starting job, even after he proved that he could play as well as anybody on the team; the quarterback competition he was forced into that led to his injury; and the fact that he was only the third-string quarterback even after he came back for the 1977 season.

Despite his troubles, Joe never gave less than his all when he did play. He resented being benched, but all of his coaches agree that he was one of the most coachable players they have ever had. Joe Montana had an uncanny ability to absorb new plays and ideas, and to immediately translate them into plays on the field.

In 1977, this ability led to a comeback victory. It was against Purdue, in the third game of

a season that the Irish had started out 1-1. With
11 minutes left, after already using two other
quarterbacks, Devine put Montana in the game.
He stepped up to the line of scrimmage with his
team trailing 24–14. It was as good as in the
bank for Purdue. Then Montana threw one
touchdown pass and handed off on another, and
Notre Dame won 31–24.

After that game, Joe Montana was the starting quarterback for the rest of his career at
Notre Dame. This paid off immediately because
Notre Dame was a contender for the national
title that year. Each passing week, the team
gained momentum. Montana avenged the loss in
his sophomore year to USC, leading the team to
a 49–12 romp over the Trojans.

In 1978, the Fighting Irish made it to the
Cotton Bowl in Dallas to play the number-one
ranked team, the University of Texas. Texas
seemed to have everything in their favor: They
had the Heisman Trophy winner (and eventual
NFL star) Earl Campbell, and Brad Shearer
had won the Outland Trophy, which was given
to the best defensive player in college football.

It should have been no contest, but Notre Dame won 38–10, capturing the national championship. Montana had lived out a dream season, even throwing a touchdown pass in the final championship game.

A Final Thrill

The next year, Notre Dame did not win the national championship, but they did return to the Cotton Bowl. This would be Joe's last game for Notre Dame, and one of his best ever.

The 1979 Cotton Bowl against the University of Houston was a classic, one of the most thrilling comebacks in the history of college football. The week of the big game did not start well for Montana. He came down with the flu. Then, to make things worse, the night before the game, an ice storm swept through Dallas. Montana was caught by surprise; the weather was more like that of Pennsylvania than what he imagined the weather in Texas would be like. The stadium was literally covered in ice. The people who did make it to the game—and almost

Montana evades Houston's Fred Snell during the 1979 Cotton Bowl. In spite of the flu and freezing weather, Montana led Notre Dame to another last-minute comeback victory. The final score was 35–34.

40,000 chose not to—had to knock the ice off of their seats before they could sit down.

Conditions on the field were even worse. Usually, the artificial turf would have been bad enough to fall down on, but now it was frozen solid. To add to the misery, a 30-mile-an-hour wind was gusting through the stadium, making it feel like 10 degrees below zero. Early on in the game, Notre Dame scored twice, with Montana taking the first touchdown in himself. Soon after that, the Irish fell apart. Houston scored 20 unanswered points. At halftime, Montana's body temperature was down to 96 degrees, and he was shaking uncontrollably. He had to be taken out of the game, and the coaches tried feeding him chicken broth to try and make him warmer. Luckily, it worked. By the end of the third quarter, Montana felt good enough to take the field. Even better, he was determined not to end his college career on a loss.

He had his work cut out for him. The Irish trailed 34–12 with seven and a half minutes left in the game. First, a blocked punt led to a Notre Dame touchdown, with Montana passing for the two-point conversion. On the next possession, he led a 61-yard drive in under two minutes, which ended when he ran the ball in himself from two yards out. But on the next drive, Montana fumbled the ball away. Luckily, the Notre Dame defense held and Joe got the ball back at the Houston 29-yard line with 28 seconds left. Working quickly, he got the team down to the eight-yard line with six seconds left. Montana tried to throw the ball to the corner of the end zone for wide receiver Kris Haines, but his throw was too low. That left two seconds to go. The next play would be the last of his college career.

What would it be? Coach Devine signaled that it was up to Montana. He called the exact same play, this time zipping it into the hands of a diving Haines. Notre Dame had pulled off another impossible comeback. It was a remarkable victory. Joe Montana had proved everything he could at the college level. It was time to move on to the pros.

The Pros

Had Joe Montana had the choice to play for any team in the National Football League, he probably would have chosen the Pittsburgh Steelers, his home-town team. The Steelers dominated the league in the 1970s by winning four Super Bowl titles, and they were still a very tough team when Montana broke into the league. Indeed, had Joe played for the Steelers, perhaps they and not the 49ers would own the league record for the most Super Bowl titles.

The Draft

However, the world of professional football did not allow Montana to choose which team he wanted to play for. For him to have a professional football career, he would have to submit to the draft and hope for the best. It meant that once again he would be examined by scouts from different teams. During the spring of 1979, Montana traveled to New York City to take part in a big tryout with many other players. He also had workouts with the Packers and the Rams.

In the meantime, he had graduated with a degree in business administration and marketing, thus fulfilling his parents' other dream for him. Although he had often struggled academically while at Notre Dame, Montana had worked hard to keep his grades up, especially when he had been forced to sit out football because of his injury. His hard work had paid off, and he graduated with a solid B average.

After graduation, Montana packed his things and moved west to Manhattan Beach, in the Los Angeles area. Maybe it was the "ice bowl" in which he had played his last game, but he was tired of cold weather. Los Angeles, in sunny southern California, seemed the perfect place to be. This was quite a change from five years before, when he had been so homesick

Forty-Niners coach Bill Walsh, shown here with Montana during the 1989 play-offs, bided his time to pick up the quarterback in the third round of the 1979 NFL draft.

that one night, he drove all the way home from Notre Dame to Monongahela. Now he was happy being on his own and looking forward to starting his pro career.

Montana first became aware that the 49ers were interested in him when Bill Walsh, the new coach and general manager of the team, came to Los Angeles to look at a running back from UCLA named James Owens. Montana went to the workout to help throw passes to Owens, but the 49ers quarterback coach, Sam Wyche (who, like many 49ers assistant coaches, would later become a head coach himself), began to test Montana more and more. It seemed that the 49ers had been interested in him all along.

Number 82

On draft day in 1979, Montana was picked by the 49ers in the third round. He was the 82nd pick in the draft. Eighty-one players were chosen ahead of him! Did nobody else see what Bill Walsh did?

Part of the reason Montana was taken so far down in the draft is that only three teams, the New York Giants, the Kansas City Chiefs, and the Chicago Bears, were in desperate need of a quarterback. The Giants took Phil Simms, who would later have many memorable duels with Montana and would help his team win two Super Bowls; the Chiefs took a strong-armed quarterback named Steve Fuller; and the Bears decided to take a running back instead. Because of this, Montana was available for Bill Walsh, who was looking for a quarterback around whom to build his team. He was so impressed by Montana's workout for him in Los

Angeles that he passed on taking Steve Dils, who had been his quarterback the year before when Walsh had coached at Stanford University.

Besides his size problems and apparent lack of arm strength, the scouts may have been worried about Montana's relationship with Dan Devine. Once a player gets tagged with the reputation of being "hard to coach," it can be difficult for him to make it in the world of football, which places a lot of emphasis on following orders. But the coaches should have noted that despite his problems with Devine, Montana had always followed coaches' instructions without argument. And, if they had asked, the coaches would have learned how much Montana was respected by his teammates and how much they believed that he could get them out of any problem.

In effect, the low pick turned out to be a blessing for Montana—the city of San Francisco, and the 49ers, would turn out to be the perfect place for him. At first glance, though, it seemed as though it could hardly have been worse.

Bottom of the Barrel

Frankly, the 49ers were a mess. They had been bad for years and were coming off a year when they had been absolutely lousy, finishing up only 2–14. This prompted their owner, Eddie DeBartolo Jr., to hire Bill Walsh, a longtime NFL assistant coach and Stanford coach for the previous two years. Walsh had a reputation for being a wizard with a team's offense, but nobody knew how he would do as head coach. As it turned out, he and Montana made a great team.

Montana was able to win a job on the team—not very surprising, considering that Walsh wanted to build the team around him. The veterans, such as O.J. Simpson, helped make him feel welcome; even the man whose job he wanted, Niners quarterback Steve DeBerg, made him feel like he belonged. He also became very close friends with his roommate, a tenth-round pick named Dwight Clark. Joe and Dwight's on-field chemistry was just as strong: Montana-to-Clark became the stuff of which legends are made.

When Montana joined the 49ers, Steve DeBerg *(above)* was their starting quarterback. DeBerg moved on, and in 1998, when he played for the Atlanta Falcons, he became the oldest starting quarterback in NFL history.

Montana saw very limited action his first year in the league. Steve DeBerg was still the Niners quarterback, a seasoned veteran with a competitiveness to match Montana's. Coach Walsh deliberately used Montana only in situations where the risk to him was low and where he could learn about quarterbacking in the NFL. Montana held the ball on field-goal and extra-point attempts, and he got some work in when the team was over their opponent's 50-yard line. Meanwhile, he was learning the system and working hard on it in practice.

The West Coast Offense

The West Coast offense is Coach Walsh's most lasting contribution to the NFL. Today, many teams use some version of it as their preferred offense. The basic theory of the West Coast offense is to use short passes to advance the ball quickly. Short passes are preferred because they have a greater chance of being caught and are less likely to be intercepted. At the same time, Coach Walsh devised many complicated pass routes for his receivers so that they would "flood" the area from 7 to 15 yards from the quarterback. This not only meant that there was a greater chance of one of them getting open and making the catch, but also that the defense would be so confused that it might not tackle the receiver, allowing him to turn a short catch into a substantial gain.

Although the West Coast offense (so named because it was first used by the Niners, who play on the West Coast) had its origin in ideas Walsh had been working on since his days as an assistant coach for the Cincinnati Bengals, it took its final form in the system he put into place for the 1981 Niners. The short passes helped to compensate for

Continued on next page

Continued from previous page

the 49ers lack of an effective ground game. In addition, Montana's trademark ability to scramble and roll out of the pocket, along with his uncanny accuracy, made him the perfect quarterback for the West Coast offense. The system also allowed him to beat quarterbacks who had more powerful arms. Still, it is strange to consider that Walsh's masterpiece of game planning was essentially designed for a rookie quarterback who didn't have a good running game to back him up.

Rising Star

In 1980, Montana saw more action, eventually starting 7 of the last 10 games the 49ers played. His roommate, Dwight Clark, was emerging as a reliable receiver as well as Joe's favorite target. Although Joe's numbers were still modest, he led the league in passing percentage at 64.5 percent. He also threw 15 touchdowns and had only 9 interceptions. He was developing confidence, and the team was improving around him, especially

Montana *(left)* replaced DeBerg *(right)* as the 49ers' starting quarterback in 1981. Delivering four world championships, he transformed the franchise from an object of ridicule to one of envy.

the offensive line. For most of Montana's career with the 49ers, he was fortunate enough to play behind an excellent offensive line. Everything he eventually did was made possible by those giants in front of him.

In a December game against New Orleans, Montana brought the Niners back from 28 points down, eventually leading them to the game-winning field goal in overtime. It was the biggest regular-season comeback in league history and a sign of things to come.

However, it looked as though Montana would once again be in a quarterback competition. Going into the 1981 season, Coach Walsh told Montana that he would be the starting quarterback. Experience made Montana doubtful. In a surprise move, Steve DeBerg was traded to the Denver Broncos. (Ironically, the durable DeBerg would still be playing when Montana retired 13 years later.) The San Francisco 49ers were now Joe Montana's team. Could this 25-year-old quarterback, who was only two years out of college, lead them to NFL greatness?

The year before, they had improved their record to 6–10, which, though not good by anyone's standards, was a definite step in the right direction. Games like the one against New Orleans promised that they would at least be entertaining to watch. There were other signs that things were going to get better. The Niners' draft picks in 1981 suddenly gave them a deep, talented, and ferocious defensive backfield; one of them, Ronnie Lott, would eventually be inducted with Joe into the Pro Football Hall of Fame.

Still, when they lost their first two games that year, most people didn't think that the Niners were headed for anything special. But then they started to win. Not only did they win, they began to beat good teams. They went to Pittsburgh and beat them 17–14. They drubbed Dallas 45–14. They kept on winning, ending up 13-3 and making the play-offs.

First they had to play the New York Giants, a team they had beaten in the regular season. There were some tense moments, but the Niners eventually pulled away, winning 38–17. This set up a famous confrontation with "America's Team," the

Ed "Too Tall" Jones of the Dallas Cowboys gets in Montana's face *(center with ball)* as he tries to make a throw.

Dallas Cowboys, who had been to a record five Super Bowls. The Cowboys were big, tough, and experienced. They had a gifted quarterback, Danny White; a Hall-of-Fame running back, Tony Dorsett; and the ferocious "Doomsday Defense," led by six-foot-nine-inch Ed "Too Tall" Jones. The Cowboys were sure of themselves; they had just beaten Tampa Bay 38–0. They had little respect for the upstart 49ers; Too Tall was quoted as saying that their record was a fluke.

They should have paid more attention to Joe Montana.

The Catch

The game was a seesaw affair. The Cowboys led 17–14 at halftime. Montana threw two touchdown passes for the San Francisco points. Both defenses clamped down in the third quarter, but the Niners broke through with a rushing touchdown to give themselves a 21–17 lead. But in the fourth quarter, the Cowboys got a quick field goal and then turned a Niners fumble at midfield into a touchdown. With about four minutes left, Joe Montana took the ball on his own 11-yard line. He was 89 yards and just more than three minutes away from history.

Working calmly, Montana led the team to the Cowboys' six-yard line. He missed his receiver on second down, leaving them with third-and-goal from the six, with 58 seconds left in the game. Montana knew he had to be careful not to give up an interception in this situation. They would still have a down to go if he failed to throw a touchdown. On third down, Montana scrambled to the right. Three Cowboys took off after him. He bought time by pumping once, and then saw Dwight Clark cutting back toward him in the end zone. He put up a high, hard pass, so that if Clark didn't catch it nobody else could.

Clark leapt up and made what is now universally known as The Catch. It was the defining moment of young Joe Montana's career, and it was the start of the 49ers' dynasty. To this day, people in San Francisco can tell you where they were when Dwight Clark made The Catch. It was the game-winning touchdown, and it put the Niners in the 1982 Super Bowl.

Their opponents were the Cincinnati Bengals, the team for which Bill Walsh had been a longtime assistant. The Bengals were led by one of his former quarterbacks, Ken Anderson, who was the All-Pro quarterback that year. Once again, people doubted the Niners' ability. They shouldn't have. In the first half, Montana scored the first touchdown himself and passed for another in building a 20–0 lead. Cincinnati made a run in the second half, but a terrific goal-line stand by the Niners' defense—the most underrated part of the team during their long run at

Montana's fourth-quarter pass to Dwight Clark *(above),* secures a last-minute 28–27 win for the 49ers against the Dallas Cowboys and a place in the 1982 Super Bowl.

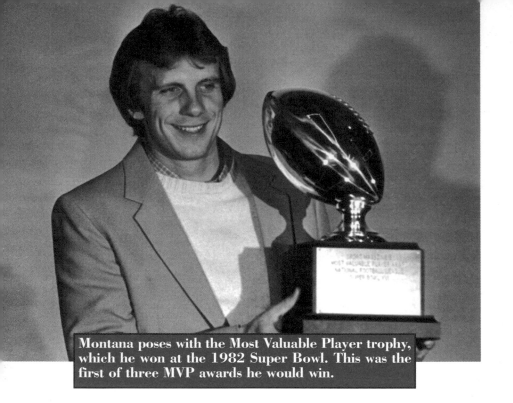

Montana poses with the Most Valuable Player trophy, which he won at the 1982 Super Bowl. This was the first of three MVP awards he would win.

the top of the NFL—stopped the Bengals cold at the San Francisco one-yard line. The final score was 26–21 San Francisco. Just four years after winning a college national championship, Joe Montana had won the world championship. He was also named Super Bowl MVP.

It was a sign of great things to come, although there would be much hardship along the way. But by the time he was done playing, Joe Montana would make the San Francisco 49ers the greatest dynasty in the history of the NFL.

Dynasty

Repeating a championship is very difficult in any sport. First of all, it's tough to keep a team together to make another championship run. Players retire, get hurt, or are traded away. Second, other teams try to improve themselves and take advantage of the weakness of the championship team.

Professional football makes it even harder for a team to defend its championship. For one thing, the schedules are designed so that the Super Bowl winner must play the toughest possible opponents. The champs also get the very last pick in the draft. Because of this, from 1979, when the Steelers won their second Super Bowl in a row and their fourth overall, to 1989, when the Niners also won their second in a row and their fourth overall, no NFL team successfully defended its title. Hence, it comes as no surprise that the 49ers did not win the Super Bowl in 1983. What disappointed their fans was how far they fell. However, by the end of the decade, the Niners would win two more Super Bowls. They would become a dynasty, and many people would begin to say that they were the greatest dynasty in the history of the NFL.

Back to Earth

There was trouble in the air as the Niners got ready to play that year. Many teams thought that the Niners had had a weak schedule and that they had gotten by on a few clutch plays in the play-offs that might have gone either way. The lack of a serious running game, usually the bedrock of a championship team, also made the Niners look vulnerable.

In addition, there were squabbles about pay raises and rumors that some of the players were using illegal drugs, though these proved to be mostly untrue. (Drug rumors would continue to haunt Montana, as we will see later.) But the most divisive issue concerning the Niners was the upcoming labor negotiations.

The Union and the Strike

The NFL players had fought long and hard to establish a union. Baseball players had called several strikes, including a long one in 1981 that had cut some 80 games from the season and had resulted in a split season. It also ended up giving them higher paychecks and a greater degree of freedom in deciding which teams they played for. Football players, on the other hand, were mostly at the mercy of team management. Almost always, their contracts were not guaranteed, meaning that if a player got hurt before his contract was up, the team did not have to pay him the rest of the money on his contract. This was also true if the team cut the player. There was no free agency in the NFL; the only way a player could go to another team was if he was traded or released by his current team.

Gene Upshaw, president of the NFL Players Association, briefs reporters on the NFL strike in 1982. The strike was one of the low points in a disastrous 1982–1983 season for Joe Montana.

The Niners got off to a bad start that year, losing their first two games. Then a strike was called. Montana and some of the players were opposed to the strike. Montana was not a member of the NFL Players Association, the players' union. He disagreed with the goals of the union leaders, who wanted a pay raise for the players and a share in the money the teams got from the television networks.

Montana wanted free agency—the right of a player to sign a contract with any team when his contract runs out—to be the players' main demand. However, many of the players on the 49ers were members of the union. To have their quarterback, the team's on-field leader, oppose the strike was very difficult for them to accept. It made for hard feelings on both sides.

The strike lasted for seven weeks before the players came back to work. The games they had missed were not made up. When play resumed, the Niners continued to stumble, going 3-6 the rest of the way. Although Montana had impressive numbers, leading the league with 17 touchdowns, the whole season was a disaster for the 49ers.

There was even more uncertainty for the 49ers going into the 1983 season. Bill Walsh was unsure whether he wanted to return to the Niners. He eventually decided to return, but some of the players were upset by how long it took him to announce his decision.

Bouncing Back

On the field, however, the Niners bounced back to a 10-6 record. They were aided by the emergence of running back Wendell Tyler, who at last gave them a legitimate ground game. Montana had an even better season than he'd had the year before, and he was clearly developing into one of the best quarterbacks in the league. The team made the play-offs and just got past the Detroit Lions to set up a confrontation with the Washington Redskins in the conference championship game. It was another wild game, but several controversial calls went against the Niners, and they ended up losing 24–21 despite a furious comeback led by Montana. The Redskins went on to lose the Super Bowl. The Niners went home with a burning ambition to win the Super Bowl the next year.

TIME

SUPERDREAMS

KILLING COLD
The U.S. Freezes Over

San Francisco's Joe Montana

Time magazine toasts Joe Montana's victory in the 1982 Super Bowl. His uncanny ability to bring a team back from apparent defeat was so frequent that it became known as Montana Magic.

The Great Years

If 1983 showed everyone that the 49ers were for real, 1984 showed that they might be one of the greatest teams in history. Their defense was rock solid. The offense kept getting better; with new running back Roger Craig, they finally had the ideal runner for Bill Walsh's system—a quick man who could catch short passes and do something big with them. They went 15-1, the first team in league history to win 15 games. The only game they lost was to Montana's hometown team, the Steelers, when he was intercepted late in the game, resulting in a game-winning field goal for Pittsburgh. Except for that play, they might well have become the first team to go undefeated since the NFL went to a 16-game schedule.

Marching through the play-offs, the 49ers got past a tough Giants team and then took on the Chicago Bears. Owners of the most formidable defense in the league, the Bears were confident that they could shut down the powerful Niners offense and move on to the Super Bowl. This angered the Niners' defense, who were a fine unit in their own right. They got a chance to shut down the opposition in a game Montana led against the Bears. The final score was 23–0, and San Francisco was back in the big game. Their next opponents were the Miami Dolphins, led by another brilliant western Pennsylvania quarterback, Dan Marino. Most people favored the Dolphins in Super Bowl XIX.

Dan Marino

If any other quarterback in the last 20 years can claim to be the greatest in the game, it is Dan Marino. In 1984, he threw a league record of 48 touchdowns; even if you count the play-offs, Montana never threw for more than 37 in any year. That year, Marino also threw for more than 5,000 yards, another record, and had four games in which he passed for more than 400 yards (and five others in which he threw for more than 390 yards). He had a great arm and was capable of getting the ball 50 yards downfield in the air, and his accuracy rivaled Montana's. He had brilliant instincts as well as one of the quickest releases in

Continued on next page

Continued from previous page

the league. Because of this, he was also one of the least-sacked quarterbacks in the NFL. Like Montana, Marino was at his best late in a game—this is where he led many incredible comebacks.

Only one thing eluded Dan Marino in his 17-year career: a Super Bowl ring. The 1985 Super Bowl against the 49ers was to be his only appearance in the NFL's title game. His Dolphins teams were always held back by their lack of a strong running game. Marino retired in 1999, holding the NFL records for the most career touchdown passes, yards, pass attempts, and pass completions. Unfortunately, he will also forever be known as the best quarterback who didn't win a Super Bowl.

Showdown at Stanford

That year, the Super Bowl game was played in Stanford Stadium, not far from San Francisco. This gave the Niners a little bit of a "home field" advantage. And Montana's competitive instincts had been fired up by all the attention being paid to Marino. Montana was determined to have a good game. It turned out to be a blowout. The Niners led 28–16 at the half and won the game 38–16. Montana had a marvelous game, throwing for 331 yards on 24-for-35 passing, including three touchdown passes. Once again, he was named the Super Bowl MVP.

Joe and Jen

As wonderful as the 1984 season was for Montana on the field, it was even better when he wasn't playing. While filming a television commercial featuring razor blades for shaving in February, 1984, Montana had met a model named Jennifer Wallace. The two hit it off immediately and began dating during the football off-season. In August, after an exhibition game, Montana took Jen to a park in San Francisco. He had hired a friend of his to fly above the park in a plane with a banner saying "Jen will you marry me? Joe" trailing after it. For a second, she didn't see the banner. Then she asked Joe what had taken him so long.

It was Montana's third marriage; he had been briefly married at the beginning of his 49ers career. He and his second wife, Cass

The 1984 season was a great one for Montana and was capped by another Super Bowl victory and his second MVP award. In 122 passes in four Super Bowls, he was never intercepted.

Castillo, whom he had married in 1979, had broken up after just a few years. The third time was the charm for Joe Montana, and he and Jennifer have two sons and two daughters.

Marriage aside, 1985 would not prove to be one of Montana's favorite years. Although he got married in the winter and his daughter, Alexandra, was born later in the year, he experienced frustration both on and off the field. First there were injuries. He had missed a game in 1984 because of a rib injury; he would miss another in 1985. A bad back limited his effectiveness, and by the time the play-offs rolled around, he would need eight painkiller injections to be able to play.

Off the field, Montana became the subject of vicious drug rumors. Totally unfounded, they dogged him the entire season. It is difficult to understand why he was singled out, but this was during the time when the nation was first coming to realize that illegal drugs were being used by many athletes. Over the summer, a trial in Pittsburgh had revealed that many prominent baseball players were using cocaine. The false rumors were a distraction that the 49ers did not need in a season in which they would lose six games by a total of only 36 points. They managed to make it into the play-offs as a wild-card team but were stopped cold by the Giants in New York, ending a season of frustration for Montana and the Niners.

His Greatest Comeback

The next season would prove to be even rougher on Montana, but he would respond with one of the most amazing comebacks in the history of sports. Joe had a condition called scoliosis, a curvature and narrowing of the spine. It had never affected him much until the opening game of the 1986 season, when he threw a pass across his body and felt something pop. He had ruptured a disk in his back, and it was more serious than normal. Montana had to have back surgery.

The two-hour operation left him with permanent numbness in one foot, and Montana had to teach himself how to walk again. Yet, in just under two months after his surgery, he returned to the

49ers' starting lineup. It was truly an astonishing display of courage and physical ability.

The Niners once again made the play-offs, with Montana leading them in the last seven games of the season, and the team advanced to the conference championship where they again met the Giants. That year, New York was not to be denied by anyone—they would eventually win the Super Bowl—and they blew out the Niners 49–3. Montana was knocked out of the game by a brutal hit from the Giants' nose tackle, Jim Burt. But Montana's back held up, proving once and for all that he was capable of playing full-time in the NFL.

Despite that, during the off-season, the Niners traded for the starting quarterback of the Tampa Bay Buccaneers, Steve Young. A talented young quarterback with remarkable running ability, Young would make an excellent backup for Montana—if that was all Young was meant to be. Montana had his doubts. It seemed that, as before, he would have to prove that he should be the starter.

Montana did not have a good relationship with Steve Young *(above)*, the 49ers' second-string quarterback who eventually replaced him.

An Unfriendly Rivalry

This became clear during the 1987 play-offs. The Minnesota Vikings were blowing out the Niners at home, and Coach Walsh pulled Montana out of the game and sent in Steve Young. Young had some success, inspiring a full-blown quarterback controversy that would last for the next five years.

In 1988, Montana missed some games and Young started in his place. There was private grumbling from people around the Niners that Young should be starting and that Montana either should be a backup or be traded before he got too old to be worth much. Few people were saying that after the 1988 season, however. After putting up only a 10-6 record, the Niners had pushed their way through the play-offs and were again facing the Cincinnati Bengals. Led by their talented left-handed quarterback, Boomer Esiason, the Bengals' "no-huddle" offense had put up impressive numbers all year. By this point, few people were willing to take the 49ers for granted, but most agreed that the Bengals had an excellent chance to beat them.

Indeed, the game was one of the best in Super Bowl history. With three minutes left in the game, the Bengals had a 16–13 lead and the Niners were backed up on their own eight-yard line. This was right where Joe Montana wanted them. Aware of the tension among the team, Montana looked for a way to lighten the mood. Glancing in the stands, he noticed actor John Candy sitting nearby. "Isn't that John Candy?" he asked in the huddle. It loosened up the team and got them ready to make what was perhaps Montana's greatest comeback of all.

The Drive

Working without a huddle, Montana kept moving the team upfield, finally reaching the Bengals' 10-yard line. Faking a pass to eventual Super Bowl MVP Jerry Rice, Montana spotted John Taylor—a superb wide receiver and the fastest man on the team—streaking toward the end zone. He hit him perfectly in stride to give the 49ers their third Super Bowl win. This comeback, known as The Drive, was perhaps the most dramatic end to any Super Bowl in history.

It was Coach Walsh's last win with the 49ers. He stepped down after the Super Bowl and George Seifert, his defensive coordinator, took over. It didn't make a difference. Shrugging off questions about his age (34) and his injuries, ignoring the rumors that he would be traded so that Steve Young could take over, Montana led the Niners right back to the Super Bowl in 1990. That time, they blew out Denver, 55–10. Montana was both the regular-season and the Super Bowl MVP. He set a Super Bowl record by throwing five touchdown passes. He and the Niners were on top of the world.

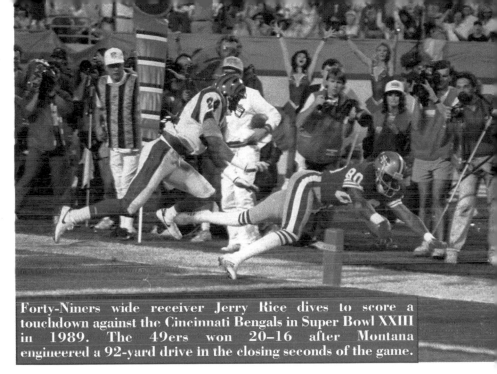

Forty-Niners wide receiver Jerry Rice dives to score a touchdown against the Cincinnati Bengals in Super Bowl XXIII in 1989. The 49ers won 20–16 after Montana engineered a 92-yard drive in the closing seconds of the game.

Montana had just experienced the best two years of his career. Most people were sure he would be selected for the Pro Football Hall of Fame after he retired. But, as Montana said in his 1995 autobiography, *Montana*, he didn't think about that while he played. "As a kid growing up, I wanted to go to Notre Dame and further than that, I wanted to be in the NFL and I wanted to win a Super Bowl," he said. "Those were all tangible things. I could go out and I could practice and I could play . . . But you can't go out and [say], 'Yeah, I made the Hall of Fame today.' That was never there."

This photograph shows 49ers wide receiver Jerry Rice and quarterback Joe Montana *(center)* being interviewed after they posted a huge 55–10 victory over the Denver Broncos in 1990, clinching Super Bowl XXIV.

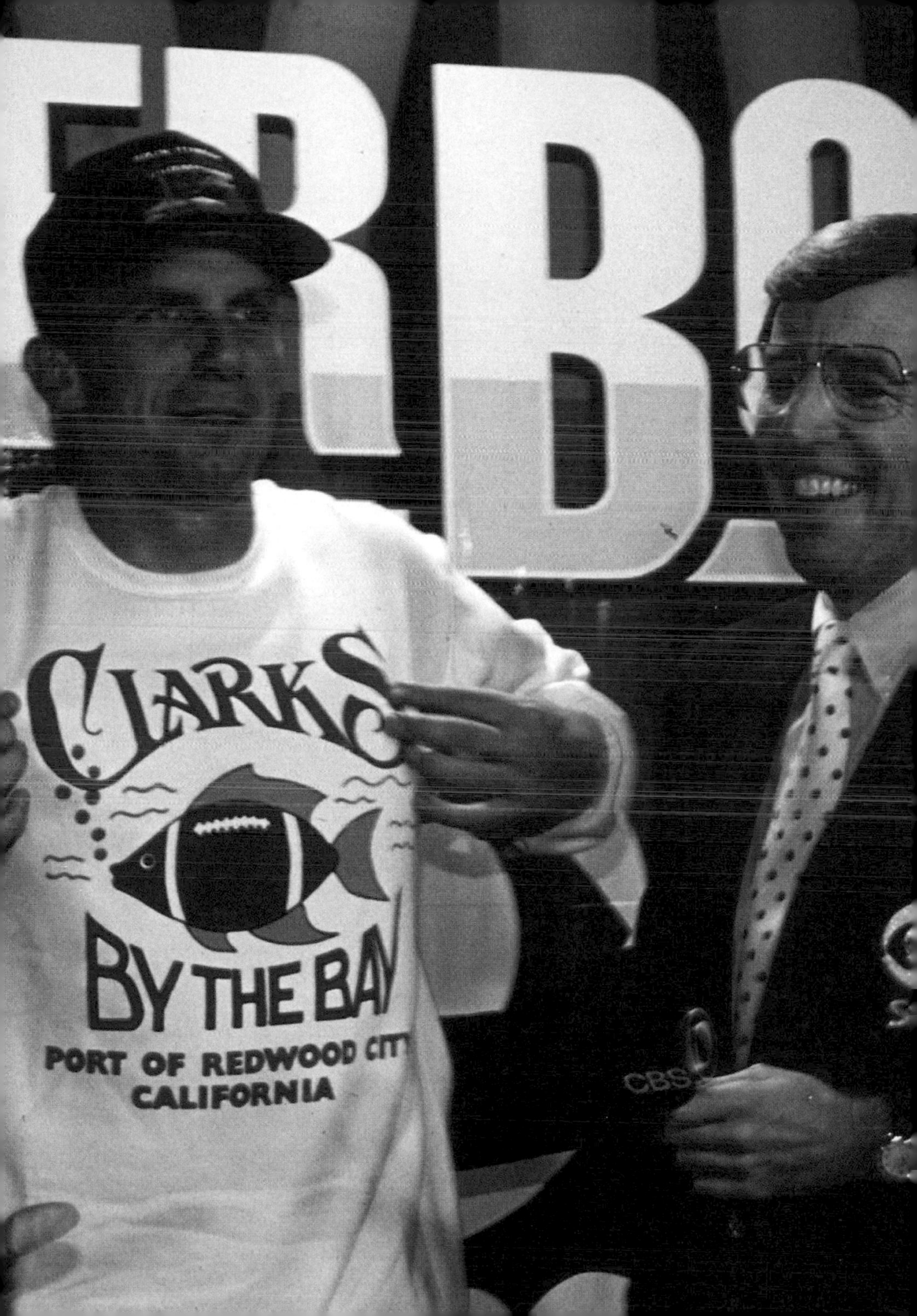
CLARKS
BY THE BAY
PORT OF REDWOOD CITY
CALIFORNIA
CBS

End of an Era

In 1990, the Niners started out the season 10-0 and cruised to the league's best record. They advanced to the conference finals, where they again faced the Giants. The Giants were no longer the dominating team they had been in 1986, but they had a core of veterans on defense— Lawrence Taylor and Leonard Marshall—who made them a very tough team to beat. In a classic defensive struggle, the Niners were clinging to a 13–12 lead when Marshall swung around completely. He unblocked and sacked Montana viciously from behind, cracking one of his ribs, bruising his sternum, and breaking his hand. (Montana insists to this day that Marshall deliberately snapped his hand back as he made the sack.) Moments later, Taylor stripped the ball out of Roger Craig's hands and the Giants kicked a 46-yard field goal as time ran out. The dream of playing in three straight Super Bowls had ended.

Montana didn't realize it at the time, but his career with the San Francisco 49ers had also ended. He would play just one more game for them.

5

The Greatest

Joe Montana had played in pain for most of his career. Groin pulls and bad knees had taken away his once above-average speed, although he remained a great scrambler. Several rib cage injuries had forced him to wear a heavy leather vest to prevent further damage to his body. He had even suffered a few concussions. And of course, there was the terrible back injury from which few people could have recovered. But he still managed to play better than any other quarterback in the game.

Years of Pain

His age and his long list of injuries were finally catching up with Montana. During training camp in 1991, Montana's right elbow was so sore that he couldn't throw the ball. In October of that year,

Montana came back from injuries to play this last game for the 49ers in 1992 against the Detroit Lions. "Joe Cool" led his team to a 24–6 victory.

he had to have surgery on the elbow, ending his season before it could start. Steve Young became the head quarterback and played very well, and the 49ers just missed making the play-offs.

The long-brewing quarterback controversy in San Francisco now came to a head. Who was to be the quarterback, Montana or Young? According to football tradition, a player shouldn't lose his job because of injury. But many felt that Young's youth, speed (he was one of the best running quarterbacks in the NFL), and superior arm strength made him a better bet. On the other hand, Montana had three Super Bowl MVP awards to his name and had led the team to four Super Bowl victories and nearly 30 comeback wins.

Then another injury sorted everything out. Again, Montana needed elbow surgery. He would miss almost the entire season. Sitting on the bench was hard for Montana to take. He turned to other diversions. He took flying lessons and bought his own small airplane to fly in, and he played a great deal of golf. He took up horseback riding and tae kwon do to help get into shape.

Montana participates in the Classic Equestrian Festival in Portolla Valley, California, in 1998. What began during his football years as an alternative way of getting in shape when he was injured, is today a major part of the former NFL star's life. He and his wife, Jennifer, train and show horses.

A tense situation was developing within the 49ers. Steve Young had an even better season in 1992, and the 49ers were strong contenders for the championship. They seemed to have become Young's team. But many on the team still wanted Montana to return to his old job. In December of 1992, he did. With the 49ers already having made the play-offs, Coach Seifert put Montana in at the start of the second half of a meaningless game against the Detroit Lions. Proving that his old magic was still intact, Montana threw for two touchdowns and looked as if he had never left. The crowd responded by cheering their hearts out for the man who had been the leader of the team for more than 10 years.

That was his last appearance in a 49ers uniform. He did not get into any play-off games, and the 49ers lost to Dallas in the conference championship game.

Good-bye, San Francisco

What happened next still makes many 49er fans bitter. First, Coach Seifert announced that even if Montana was healthy next year, Steve Young was his quarterback. Based on the numbers, this decision made sense. However, not everyone was happy with this. Many fans wanted Montana to return; so did some of his teammates. However, Montana made it clear that he was not interested in being a backup quarterback, and he asked the 49ers to trade him. Which team he would end up with soon became a hot topic around the country. At the same time, some people who ran the 49ers felt that they should keep Montana in town and let him finish his career as a Niner.

Meanwhile, Montana was trying to find a team that he wanted to play on and that would pay him what he wanted. It would be the final contract of his career. The two main contenders were the Phoenix Cardinals and the Kansas City Chiefs. At the last minute, the 49ers offered to make Montana the starting quarterback and let him end his career with them. But it was too late. Montana's pride had been hurt by Seifert's lack of support. Without the coach behind him, Montana knew he was just one bad play away from being benched and reigniting a

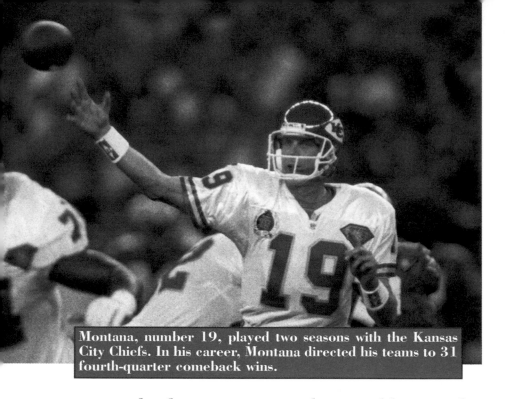

Montana, number 19, played two seasons with the Kansas City Chiefs. In his career, Montana directed his teams to 31 fourth-quarter comeback wins.

quarterback controversy that could tear the team apart. In any case, Montana had already decided on his next destination. Although the Cardinals had offered him more money, he accepted the Chiefs' offer for a simple reason: They had a chance to win a Super Bowl.

Hello, Kansas City

For several seasons, Kansas City had been a strong team, making the play-offs but unable to advance very far. The core of the team was its powerful defense, anchored by Neil Smith and

Derrick Thomas (who would tragically die in a car accident several years later). The offense had been the team's weak spot; it lacked a star quarterback and a consistent running game. Two veteran newcomers, Joe Montana and former Raiders running back Marcus Allen, hoped to fix those problems.

It wasn't going to be easy. Although Kansas City had a few promising receivers, Montana had nothing like the group he had played with in San Francisco: Dwight Clark, Brent Jones, John Taylor, and Jerry Rice, probably the greatest receiver in the history of football. And although Marcus Allen had an excellent season, proving that the Raiders had made a mistake not only in giving him up but in not using him much in the last few seasons, he was no longer capable of carrying the entire offensive load.

Montana's injuries were another problem. They limited him to only 11 games in 1993. Many wondered if he would be able to take the pounding of a full season. But he passed for more than 2,000 yards and led the Chiefs to an 11-5 record, including one more fourth-quarter come-from-behind victory, against the San Diego Chargers. He was the AFC Offensive Player of the Week twice. Not bad for a 37-year-old quarterback after major arm surgery.

In the play-offs, Montana led the Chiefs to the conference championship game against the Buffalo Bills. The winner would go to the Super Bowl, a destination Montana had reached four times before. Over in the NFC, the 49ers were to play Dallas. If both the Niners and the Chiefs won, it would set up a Super Bowl showdown between Joe Montana and Steve Young. Sadly, it was not to be. Swarmed by Buffalo's own impressive defense, Montana suffered a concussion in the third quarter and had to leave the game. Buffalo won and went to its fourth consecutive Super Bowl and its fourth consecutive Super Bowl loss, losing to Dallas for the second year in a row.

One Last Try

Montana thought about retiring after that year, but he couldn't leave without taking one last crack at reaching the Super Bowl. One other game may have interested him as well:

One for the Road

Montana also had one more special comeback left for football fans all across the country during his last season. In the sixth game of the year, on October 17, 1994, he and the Broncos' John Elway hooked up for a classic match-up in Denver's Mile High Stadium. The game was broadcast around the country on *Monday Night Football*. Both quarterbacks were in fine form, leading each other's teams up and down the field. They totaled 83 passes between them. With a minute and a half left in the fourth quarter, Elway ran the ball in himself from the four-yard line. Montana then led another memorable drive, going 75 yards in only nine plays. On the drive, Montana was six for seven in passing attempts. He ran the offense without a huddle, hurrying his teammates up to the line of scrimmage and then calmly passing the ball to them. On the last play of the drive, he saw wide receiver Willie Davis at the goal line. Davis made the catch and dove into the end zone with just eight seconds left in the game. The Chiefs had pulled out a great 31–28 win, the last of Joe's spectacular comebacks.

the second game of the season, when the San Francisco 49ers (and Steve Young) were coming to Kansas City. That game would attract the second-largest crowd in Kansas City history, and the crowd was thrilled to see the old master pull out a 24–17 win over the Niners. Young was sacked four times and also gave up the ball four times, twice on fumbles and twice throwing interceptions. It was to be the only time the two would face each other.

Sadly, there were not enough moments like that one. In a bad loss to Buffalo, Montana was sacked three times. As noted in *Montana*, after one hit by the veteran defensive end Bruce Smith—who had given him a concussion in the conference championship the year before—Montana told him, "I'm too old for this." He was 38, and his nagging injuries were bothering him. A sprained knee cost him two games and required surgery in the off-season. He managed to get the Chiefs into the play-offs with two straight wins in the last two games, leading to a first-round match-up with the Miami Dolphins and Dan Marino. Ten years before, Montana and the Niners had soundly beaten Marino and the Dolphins in the Super Bowl. But that day, the Dolphins won, eliminating the Chiefs from the play-offs and ending Montana's dream of one more Super Bowl ring. The last pass of his career was an interception, an odd ending for the man who had been the most accurate passer in history. That year, the 49ers finally made it back to the Super Bowl, winning for the fifth time. Steve Young broke Montana's record for the most touchdown passes in a Super Bowl game.

After the season, Montana announced his retirement. The time had come. For the first time, football felt like a job to him. Years of pounding had left him with some permanent injuries, such as numbness in one foot. He wanted to take more time to be with his family and to relax after many years of hard work.

He and Jennifer bought an estate in California's Napa Valley area, a region noted for its wine production. Their beautiful house is a refuge from the outside world, where Montana is still easily recognized and often mobbed by fans. At home, he can relax by cooking, playing golf,

The Comeback Kid smiles during a ceremony in which the 49ers retired his jersey number, 16, in 1997. He won the NFL's passing title in both 1987 and 1989. He topped the NFC in passing five times (1981, 1984, 1985, 1987, and 1989). Thirty-nine times he passed for more than 300 yards.

riding his horses, or swimming. He remains fit and active. For a while, he was a football announcer on television, but he has since given that up. He has remained active by doing promotional work, and he started his own investment service for professional athletes.

Joe Cool: Hall of Famer

On July 29, 2000, 18,000 people gathered in Canton, Ohio, site of the Pro Football Hall of Fame, to witness the induction of Joe Montana. The largest crowd in the history of the Hall of Fame, they saw something that had never happened on the football field: Joe Montana showing his emotions. "We seem cool and calm on the outside, but on the inside, we're a mess," he said of himself and athletes in general, as quoted from CNNSI.com (http://sportsillustrated.cnn.com).

Inducted with his Niners teammate, safety Ronnie Lott, Montana was visibly moved during the ceremony. He thanked the fans for their support and his teammates for making everything possible. He reminisced about playing against Lott during practices that got almost as intense as the actual games.

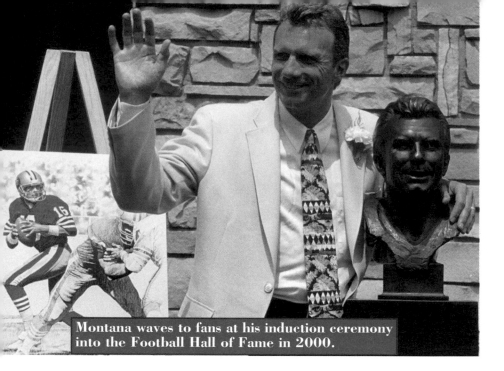

Montana waves to fans at his induction ceremony into the Football Hall of Fame in 2000.

Accompanied by Jen and his children, as well as his parents (now retired and living in San Francisco), Montana revealed how hard it had been for someone as competitive as he was to give up his career. But being named to the Hall of Fame had actually helped him adjust to retirement, Montana said in his induction speech, according to CNNSI.com (http://sportsillustrated.cnn.com). Montana said, "I had a very difficult time with it in the beginning . . . because I think I was looking at it from the wrong perspective. I looked at it like an ending point, like I was in my grave and they were throwing dirt on me and I'm trying to get out.

Joe Montana signs a momento for a child during a visit to Target House, a hotel for ill kids, in Memphis, Tennessee, in 2001.

"But then I got the meaning of it. This is not an ending point. This is a beginning point. This is a new team I'm joining. And take a look at these guys. What a team it is."

It had been a long journey for Montana, from the evenings he spent as a child throwing a football around with his father in western Pennsylvania to the top of the NFL. But those days and the lessons Montana learned from his father—not to give up, to give his all for his team, and to make the most of every opportunity—had helped him become the greatest quarterback in NFL history.

Timeline

1956 Born in New Eagle, Monongahela Valley, western Pennsylvania.

1964 Starts playing Pee Wee Football a year earlier than officially allowed.

1972 Leads Ringgold High School to a tie against rivals.

1973 Leads Ringgold to 8-1 record and is offered scholarships to college in both football and basketball.

1974 Enters the University of Notre Dame.

1975 Leads Notre Dame to two stunning comebacks but cannot capture the starting job.

1976 Sits out a year with a shoulder injury.

1978 Leads Notre Dame to the national championship, beating Texas in the Cotton Bowl.

1979 In his last game for Notre Dame—the 1979 Cotton Bowl—leads another comeback despite freezing conditions. Drafted in the third round by the San Francisco 49ers, the 82nd selection overall.

1980 Starts 7 of the last 10 games of the season, including a win over New Orleans in the biggest comeback in NFL history.

1981 Named as starting quarterback for the first time and leads San Francisco to their first Super Bowl victory. Throws The Catch to Dwight Clark against the Cowboys in the NFC championship game.

1982 Opposes the six-game NFL Players Association strike, causing dissension in the team.

1984 The Niners go 15-1 and win the Super Bowl, beating Dan Marino's Dolphins in a battle of future Hall of Famers.

1985 Marries Jennifer, his third wife. Their first daughter is born. Montana is dogged by false drug rumors.

1986 Suffers devastating back injury that requires surgery. Returns at the end of the season and leads Niners to the conference championship before losing to the eventual champions, the New York Giants.

1988 Leads Niners to third Super Bowl, beating the Cincinnati Bengals with The Drive, a last-minute 92-yard touchdown drive.

1989 The Niners win the Super Bowl again. Montana beats another future Hall of Famer, John Elway, in the most lopsided Super Bowl in history.

1990 Once again, San Francisco has the best record in the league but loses to the Giants in the conference game in what was to be Montana's last play-off game with the Niners.

1991 Elbow injury forces Montana to sit out the entire year. Steve Young takes over. The Niners fail to make the play-offs.

1992 Montana's elbow again sidelines him most of the year. He returns to play the second half of the last game of the year, his final appearance in a San Francisco uniform.

1993 Joins the Kansas City Chiefs and, despite missing several games, leads them to the AFC championship game, losing to Buffalo.

1994 In his final year in the NFL, Montana leads one more great comeback on *Monday Night Football*, beating the Broncos in Mile High Stadium. The Chiefs make the play-offs but lose to the Dolphins. Montana's final pass is intercepted.

1995 Retires and moves to California's Napa Valley.

2000 Inducted into the Pro Football Hall of Fame on the first ballot, along with longtime teammate Ronnie Lott.

Glossary

audible A new play called by the quarterback at the line of scrimmage after he decides against the original play.

backfield The area behind the line of scrimmage, or the players (offensive or defensive) who start each play there—the running backs and the quarterback, or the safeties and cornerbacks.

conference A grouping of teams in college or professional football. The NFL has two conferences, the National Football Conference (NFC), in which the San Francisco 49ers play, and the American Football Conference (AFC), in which the Kansas City Chiefs play. Each NFL conference has three divisions in it.

conference championship A play-off game that determines which team will advance from each conference to play each other in the Super Bowl.

defensive back A player, such as a safety or cornerback, that plays in the defensive backfield.

defensive end A player on the end of the defensive line whose primary job is to try to hit the quarterback.

defensive line Three or four players who line up at the line of scrimmage and are the team's first line of defense.

down On each possession, a team has four chances to try to gain ten yards. Each chance is called a down. Once the team has moved at least 10 yards, it gets another four chances to advance. Downs are usually referred to by their number and the yards needed: first-and-ten, third-and-seven, and so on. Also, a player who is tackled with the ball is said to be downed.

end zone The two areas at either end of the field, which each team tries to defend. If a team gets the ball into the other team's end zone, the team gets a touchdown.

extra point After a touchdown, an additional point scored by kicking the ball through the uprights in the same way as a field goal.

field goal A play in which the ball is kicked between the uprights over the opposition's end zone. Results in three points for the team that kicks the ball.

free agency The ability of a player to negotiate with any team he chooses when his current contract runs out.

fumble When a player who has the ball drops it. The other team can try to pick it up and gain possession of the ball.

ground game A team's rushing attack. A strong rushing game is usually needed for a team to do well.

interception A pass meant for the offense but caught by the defense. Results in the offensive team losing possession of the ball to the defensive team.

linebacker Three or four defensive players who play just behind the defensive line.

line of scrimmage A place on the field where the ball is placed before each down.

National Football League (NFL) The professional football league in the United States.

offensive line Five players in front of the quarterback whose responsibility is to protect him while he throws the ball, or to open up a space through which the running back can run.

pass A play where one player throws the ball to another; the primary job of the quarterback.

pocket The area where a quarterback is protected by his defensive players.

possession When a team is on offense, it is said to be in possession of the ball. A change of possession occurs after one team scores, after a fumble or interception, or if the team cannot advance 10 yards after four downs. A possession also refers to the series of plays a team runs before it scores or gives the ball to the other team.

punt When a team on its fourth down does not think that they can make a first down and drop-kicks the ball to the other team.

quarterback An offensive player who stands just behind the offensive line. A play starts when the ball is snapped to him. He can try to pass the ball, hand it off to another player to run with it, or run himself.

running back An offensive player whose job is to run with the ball.

rush An attempt to run with the ball instead of passing it.

short pass A pass that is caught less than 10 yards from the line of scrimmage. Generally, a short pass is a much easier play to make than a longer pass.

Super Bowl The NFL's championship game, held each year toward the end of January in a stadium selected so that bad weather will not interfere with the game.

tight end A receiver who starts at one end of the offensive line. Must be a good blocker.

touchdown A play in which a team gets the ball into its opponent's end zone, scoring six points.

turnover A play that results in the offensive team giving the ball up to the defensive team.

two-point conversion After a touchdown, two points can be scored by throwing or running the ball into the end zone from the two-yard line. It has been a part of college football for a long time, but it was only introduced to the NFL in 1994.

wide receiver An offensive player whose main job is to catch passes from the quarterback.

For More Information

Associations

College Football Hall of Fame
111 South St. Joseph Street
South Bend, IN 46601
(800) 440-FAME (3263)
Web site: http://www.hof@collegefootball.org

The National Collegiate Athletic Association
700 West Washington Street
P.O. Box 6222
Indianapolis, IN 46206-6222
(317) 917-6222
Web site: http://www.ncaa.org

The National Football League, Inc.
280 Park Avenue
New York, NY 10017
(212) 450-2000
Web site: http://www.nfl.com

Pro Football Hall of Fame
2121 George Halas Drive NW
Canton, OH 44708
(330) 456-8207
Web site: http://www.profootballhof.com

University of Notre Dame
Notre Dame, IN 46556
(219) 631-5000
Web site: http://www.nd.edu

Web Sites

Due to the changing nature of Internet links, the
Rosen Publishing Group, Inc., has developed an
online list of Web sites related to the subject of
this book. This site is updated regularly. Please
use this link to access the list:

http://www.rosenlinks.com/fhf/jmon/

For Further Reading

Christopher, Matt. *Great Moments in Football History*. Boston: Little, Brown & Company, 1997.

Dickey, Glenn. *Glenn Dickey's 49ers: The Rise, Fall, and Rebirth of the NFL's Greatest Dynasty*. Rocklin, CA: Prima Communications, Inc., 2000.

Garner, Joe, and Ara Parseghian. *Echoes of Notre Dame Football: Great and Memorable Moments of the Fighting Irish*. Naperville, IL: Sourcebooks MediaFusion, 2001.

Mandell, Ted, and Doug Flutie. *Heart Stoppers and Hail Marys: 100 of the Greatest College Football Finishes (1970–1999)*. South Bend, IN: Diamond Communications, Incorporated, 2000.

McDonough, Will, et al. *The NFL Century: The Complete Story of the National Football League, 1920–2000*. New York: U.S. Media Holdings, Inc., 2001.

Murphy, Austin. *The Super Bowl: Sport's Greatest Championship*. New York: Time Inc., 1998.

National Football League. *Official Rules of the NFL*. Chicago: Triumph Books, 2001.

Nelson, Julie, and Loren Stanley. *San Francisco 49ers*. Mankato, MN: The Creative Company, 2000.

Whittingham, Richard. *Rites of Autumn: The Story of College Football*. New York: The Free Press, 2001.

Bibliography

Kavanagh, Jack. *Sports Great Joe Montana.*
   Berkeley Heights, NJ: Enslow Publishers,
   Inc., 1992.

Kindred, Dave. "The Best." *The Sporting News,*
   Vol. 219, No. 17, April 24, 1995, p. 71.

Kindred, Dave. "The Best There Ever Was."
   The Sporting News, Vol. 223, No. 2, Jan.
   11, 1999, p. 621.

Montana, Joe, and Bob Raissman. *Audibles:
   My Life in Football.* New York: William
   Morrow and Company, Inc., 1986.

Montana, Joe, and Dick Schaap. *Montana.*
   Atlanta, GA: Turner Publishing, Inc., 1995.

Plaschke, Bill. "The Bottom Line." *The
   Sporting News,* Vol. 219, No. 17, April
   24, 1995, p. 167.

Raber, Thomas R. *Joe Montana, Comeback Quarterback*. Minneapolis: Lerner Publications Co., 1989.

Silver, Michael. "All Hail the King." *Sports Illustrated*, Vol. 82, No. 16, April 24, 1995, p. 168.

Silver, Michael. "Together Forever." *Sports Illustrated*, Vol. 93, No. 4, July 24, 2000, p. 56.

Sullivan, George. *All About Football*. New York: Dodd Mead, 1987.

Zimmerman, Paul. "Born to Be a Quarterback Part I of II." *Sports Illustrated*, Vol. 73, No. 6, August 1990, pp. 62–76.

Zimmerman, Paul. "The Ultimate Winner Part II of II," *Sports Illustrated*, Vol. 73, No. 13, August 1990, pp. 72–88.

Index

About the Author

Fred Ramen is a writer and computer programmer in New York City. A New York Giants fan, Mr. Ramen can remember where he was in 1990 when the Giants beat the Niners to reach the Super Bowl. Mr. Ramen was a semifinalist in the 1997 *Jeopardy!* Tournament of Champions.

Photo Credits

Cover, pp. 10, 12, 21, 28–29, 42, 46, 55, 75, 80, 82–83, 86, 92, 95 © AP/ Wide World Photos; pp. 4, 14 (top left and right, bottom left), 17, 31, 37, 49, 56, 60 © Bettmann/Corbis; p. 6 © Andy Hayt/ Timepix; pp. 14 (bottom right), 72 © S. Carmona/ Corbis; p. 25 © Duomo/Corbis; pp. 52, 76–77 © John W. McDonough/Icon SMI; p. 63 © Timepix; p. 68 © Wally McNamee/Corbis; p. 94 © Reuters New Media Inc./Corbis.

Design and Layout

Tahara Hasan